A TRUE BOOK™

The Seven Continents

South America

GLORIA SUSANA ESQUIVEL

Children's Press®
An Imprint of Scholastic Inc.

Content Consultant

Joseph J. García, Ph.D., Professor of Latin American & Caribbean Studies

Library of Congress Cataloging-in-Publication Data

Names: Esquivel, Gloria Susana, author.

Title: South America / by Gloria Susana Esquivel.

Description: New York, NY : Children's Press, an imprint of Scholastic Inc., 2019. | Series: A true book | Includes bibliographical references and index.

Identifiers: LCCN 2018028049| ISBN 9780531128107 (library binding : alk. paper) | ISBN 9780531134184 (pbk. : alk. paper)

Subjects: LCSH: South America—Juvenile literature.

Classification: LCC F2208.5 .E87 2019 | DDC 980—dc23

LC record available at https://lccn.loc.gov/2018028049

SCHOLASTIC, CHILDREN'S PRESS, A TRUE BOOK™, and associated logos are trademarks and/or registered trademarks of Scholastic Inc.

Scholastic Inc., 557 Broadway, New York, NY 10012

1 2 3 4 5 6 7 8 9 10 R 28 27 26 25 24 23 22 21 20 19

Front: South America

Back: Llama overlooking Machu Picchu in Peru

Find the Truth!

Everything you are about to read is true *except* for one of the sentences on this page.

Which one is **TRUE**?

T or F South America has the driest desert in the world.

T or F Italian conquistadors were the first Europeans to arrive in South America and colonize its territory.

Find the answers in this book.

Contents

THE BIG TRUTH!

Amazon in Danger

Golden lion
tamarin

Machu Picchu

Colombian artifact

Central America

Caribbean Sea

Caracas

VENEZUELA

GUYANA

SURINAME

French Guiana (FRANCE)

Orinoco River

COLOMBIA

Equator

Galápagos Is. (Ecuador)

ECUADOR

Negro River

Amazon River

Amazon River

Madiera River

Xingu River

B R A Z I L

São Francisco River

Machu Picchu, Peru

Lima ✪

PERU

L. Titicaca

BOLIVIA

Brasília ✪

PACIFIC OCEAN

PARAGUAY

CHILE

Paraná River

ATLANTIC OCEAN

← *Easter I. (Chile)*
2000 mi

Juan Fernández Is. (Chile)

Buenos Aires ✪

ARGENTINA

Río de la Plata

URUGUAY

Falkland Is.
(Islas Malvinas)
(administered
by the U.K., claimed
by Argentina)

| 0 | | 300 MI |
| 0 | | 500 KM |

Tierra del Fuego

N
W   E
S

Continent Close-up

Rio de Janeiro, Brazil

South America is the fourth-largest of Earth's seven continents. It stretches from Point Gallinas on the northern coast of Colombia down to icy Cook Island near Antarctica. South America's wide variety of **climates** and **biomes** provides the continent with some of the greatest diversity on Earth. The continent includes 12 independent countries. It also contains French Guiana, a region of France, and the Falkland Islands, which are governed by the United Kingdom.

Land area	6.8 million square miles (17.6 million square kilometers)
Number of independent countries	12
Estimated population (2017)	422.5 million
Main languages	Portuguese, Spanish, Quechua
Largest country	Brazil
Smallest country	Suriname
Fast fact	South America has two fully landlocked countries. Neither Paraguay nor Bolivia has access to an ocean.

More than half the people who visit Torres del Paine National Park are foreign tourists.

The mountains of Chile's Torres del Paine National Park offer breathtaking views to hikers.

CHAPTER 1

Land and Climate

South America contains a diverse and beautiful landscape. The western part is occupied by the Andes Mountains. These peaks run along the Pacific Coast like a gigantic backbone. The eastern part of South America contains lowlands. Here, huge rivers such as the Amazon snake through deserts, hills, forests, and fields.

Highs and Lows

The Andes is the longest mountain range in the world. They extend for about 5,500 miles (8,851 km) and range from 120 to 430 miles (193 to 692 km) wide. The Andes go through seven countries from north to south: Venezuela, Colombia, Ecuador, Peru, Bolivia, Argentina, and Chile. They contain very high **plateaus** where three main capital cities are located. Bogotá, Colombia; Quito, Ecuador; and La Paz, Bolivia, are the highest capitals in the world!

SOUTH AMERICA'S TERRAIN

Central America

Llanos

Equator

Amazon Basin

Andes Mountains

Gran Chaco

Brazilian Highlands

PACIFIC OCEAN

ATLANTIC OCEAN

Aconcagua

Pampas

KEY

TERRAIN

Ice   Mountains   Hills   Lowlands

SOUTHERN OCEAN

Tierra del Fuego

This map shows where South America's higher and lower areas are.

About 150 mammal species live in the Gran Chaco.

Sprawling cattle ranches are a common sight throughout Argentina, which is famous for its high-quality beef.

Another main geographic region is the Gran Chaco, or Chaco Plain. It is located in the lowlands of the Río de la Plata. It extends through parts of Bolivia, Paraguay, and Argentina. The Gran Chaco covers 250,000 square miles (647,497 sq km) and has some of the highest temperatures in South America. Dry thorn forests, cactus stands, and grasslands that flood in the wet season are some of the different biomes that extend through this area.

Ocean Waters

South America is bordered by the Pacific Ocean on the west and the Atlantic Ocean on the east. The Caribbean Sea is considered part of the Atlantic. Both Colombia and Venezuela lie along the Caribbean. The Gulf of Darién is the southernmost region of the Caribbean Sea. It lies between Panama and Colombia. This natural border divides North and South America.

Many tourists visit the Caribbean coast of South America because of its weather.

The Amazon rain forest is sometimes called the lungs of the world because it has so many trees, and trees produce oxygen.

Rivers and Lakes

South America has many rivers and lakes. The Amazon is the continent's most important river. With a length of 4,000 miles (6,437 km), it is the second-longest river in the world. It begins in the Andean lakes of Peru and runs its course through the low plains of Colombia and Brazil. Finally, it empties into the Atlantic Ocean.

Climate

Because South America is so large, it gets a lot of different weather. In the southern part of the continent, hot summers last from November to February. Icy winters span from June to August. The northern part of the continent is close to Earth's equator. Here, it is hot and sunny all year long. South America has the wettest and the driest places in the world. Tutunendo, Colombia, receives 449 inches (1,140 centimeters) of rainfall each year. On the other hand, Chile's Atacama Desert gets just 0.6 inch (1.5 cm) per year!

RECORD TEMPERATURES

HIGHEST	LOWEST
Rivadavia, Salta Province, Argentina, in December 1905	Sarmiento, Chubut Province, Argentina, in June 1907
120°F	-27°F
49°C	-33°C

The Atacama Desert lies along the Pacific Coast in Chile, west of the Andes Mountains.

The Angel Falls

Considered among the most extraordinary natural wonders of the world, the Angel Falls are Earth's highest uninterrupted waterfalls. Located in Canaima National Park in Venezuela, they are 3,211 feet (979 meters) tall and have a plunge of 2,648 feet (807 m). It is very difficult to travel to the Angel Falls. They are located deep in the middle of the rain forest, with no roads leading to them. They are accessible only by air.

The Angel Falls are named after Jimmie Angel, an American pilot who was the first to fly over the waterfalls.

Red-breasted toucans rest on a tree in Brazil.

More than 40 toucan species live in the Amazon.

CHAPTER 2

Plants and Animals

Dense tropical rain forests, deserts that are cold and filled with salt, and sprawling green plains are just some of the biomes in South America. Temperature, rainfall, sunlight, and physical barriers are the main factors that determine a biome. Each South American biome is home to thousands of incredible plants and animals. These species are perfectly suited for their homes.

The Venezuelan red howler monkey is famous for its incredibly loud calls.

Earth's Lungs

The Amazon rain forest is the largest tropical rain forest in the world. Located in Brazil, Peru, and Colombia, it fills 2,123,562 square miles (5,500,000 sq km). It represents over half of Earth's rain forests and has an estimated 390 billion trees. One in 10 known species in the world lives in the Amazon. This means the Amazon has the largest collection of plants and animals in the world!

Tropical Savannas

Savannas are grasslands that contain scattered trees and shrubs. Tropical savannas are found in northern South America (Venezuela, Colombia, Brazil, Guyana, and Suriname). These vast tropical plains are covered with grasses, and palm clusters grow along streams. The tropical savannas are the home of many species of reptiles and amphibians such as snakes and frogs. The capybara, a large rodent, is also found in this biome.

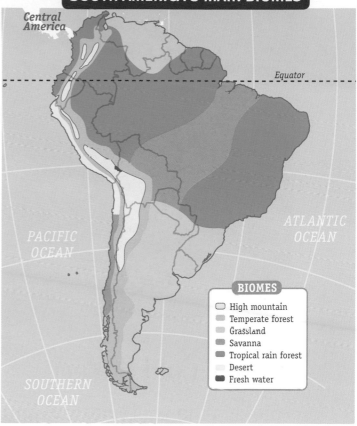

SOUTH AMERICA'S MAIN BIOMES

Central America

Equator

PACIFIC OCEAN

ATLANTIC OCEAN

SOUTHERN OCEAN

BIOMES
- High mountain
- Temperate forest
- Grassland
- Savanna
- Tropical rain forest
- Desert
- Fresh water

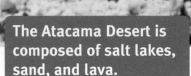

The Atacama Desert is composed of salt lakes, sand, and lava.

A Very Cold Desert

Found in the southwestern part of South America, the Atacama Desert covers a strip of land on the Pacific coast that is 600 miles (966 km) long. It is one of the driest and coldest deserts in the world! It is so dry that its soil has been compared with the soil found on Mars. Despite its harsh weather, many species of plants live here. Lizards, iguanas, and foxes also call this place home.

Gigantic Mountains

The Andes Mountains host a very diverse biome. Throughout the Andes, the climate varies, because some parts are nearer to the equator than others. The northern region is hotter and has many rain forests. In the southern region, the mountains are colder because they are closer to Antarctica. The central region has **temperate** weather. Condors, llamas, and spectacled bears are a few of the amazing animals that live in the central region.

A llama looks out over the famous ruins of Machu Picchu in Peru.

Pumas can jump incredibly long distances. This skill helps them capture prey and climb mountains.

The Green Pampas

The pampas are a region of fertile grasslands located in the southern part of South America. Covering 289,577 square miles (750,000 sq km), they cross through Argentina, Uruguay, and Brazil. Because the biome is covered with grass, many of the animals that live there are plant eaters. However, there are also predators that live here. Among them are pumas, wolves, and foxes.

Species in Trouble

Many of South America's plant and animal species are in danger of dying out, mainly due to human activities. Here are just a few:

Golden Lion Tamarin

Home: Atlantic forest of Brazil

This furry monkey is rapidly losing its **habitat** as people cut down trees in South America's forests.

Galápagos Giant Tortoise

Home: Galápagos Islands

Non native goats were introduced to the tortoise's habitat and are leaving the tortoise without enough food to eat.

Waved Albatross

Home: Galápagos Islands

These birds are unique to the Galápagos Islands. They are threatened by climate change and overfishing, which leaves them without enough food.

Amazonian Manatee

Home: Amazon River

This aquatic mammal is threatened by habitat loss and mercury pollution from illegal gold mining.

Orinoco Crocodile

Home: Orinoco River in Venezuela and Colombia

Considered the largest predator in South America, this crocodile almost disappeared during the 19th century due to demand for crocodile leather.

Amazon in Danger

Timeline

In the 1970s, deforestation in the Brazilian Amazon began to increase when highways opened deep into the forest.

Between 2001 and 2012, 3.5 million acres (1.4 million hectares) of the Amazon rain forest were lost, mostly in Brazil and Peru.

In 2015, demand for products like palm oil and soybeans led to an increase in illegal deforestation.

1970

2001–2012

201

The trees in the massive Amazon rain forest are very important to the health of the planet. We need trees to keep our air clean and breathable. But there is a problem. In the last 40 years, the Amazon has lost 18 percent of its trees. The area these trees once covered was almost as big as the entire state of California! The trees have been lost to illegal logging and cleared away to make room for soybean farms and cattle ranches.

The World Wide Fund for Nature estimates that more than a quarter of the Amazon rain forest will be without trees by 2030.

2030

Deforestation also contributes to global climate change. This major environmental issue is causing problems for many plant and animal species around the world, such as Spix's night monkey.

Originally introduced to South America by British workers, bowler hats have been popular among Bolivian women for many decades.

Bolivian dancers celebrate the annual Fiesta de la Virgen de la Candelaria in the town of Copacabana.

CHAPTER 3

A Peek at the Past

It is believed that the first humans in South America originally came from Asia. These people traveled first to North America, then **migrated** to the south. The earliest evidence of human population in South America was found in Monte Verde, Chile. It dates to about 14,000 years ago. The descendants of these first inhabitants became the **indigenous** populations of South America. Some of these cultures still exist today, especially in Bolivia and Peru.

This artifact of the Muisca people depicts a ceremony in which a new leader was covered in gold dust and sent down a river aboard a raft.

Early People

By the 1490s, when the first Europeans arrived on the continent, 60 million people lived in South America. Some of these groups had formed permanent settlements throughout the continent. The Muiscas, in Colombia, the Valdivias in Ecuador, and the Quechuas and Aymaras in Peru and Bolivia were four of the most important groups of this era. Evidence shows that they all used advanced farming techniques.

A Quechua group called the Incas ruled an empire that extended from Ecuador to Chile. Between 1438 and 1471, they conquered these territories and established their capital in Cuzco. The Incas were excellent stoneworkers. The Inca fortress Machu Picchu is evidence of their amazing architecture. Today, tourists can visit Cuzco and Machu Picchu to get a breathtaking view of what Inca civilization looked like.

Many indigenous groups in South America created beautiful sculptures of gold.

Conquistadors and Slaves

In 1498, explorer Christopher Columbus arrived in South America. In the following years, Spanish and Portuguese **conquistadors** explored the continent and enslaved its people. The Europeans brought diseases that killed almost half of the indigenous people. They also brought African slaves to work alongside the remaining natives.

South America's Timeline

12,000 BCE
By this time, the first people have arrived in South America.

1498 CE
Christopher Columbus journeys to South America, beginning the European colonization of the continent.

1721
In Paraguay, South Americans rise up against Spanish rule during the Revolt of the Comuneros.

| 12,000 BCE | 1498 CE | 1518 | 1721 |

1518
The Europeans begin bringing enslaved Africans to South America.

The enslaved people of South America tried to fight back against the Spanish and Portuguese governments. However, it was not until the early 19th century that the Spanish **colonies** won their independence. Simón Bolívar, José de San Martín, and Bernardo O'Higgins led the independence struggle across the continent. Bolívar wanted to unify the northern part of the continent as one nation, but instead several new countries were formed.

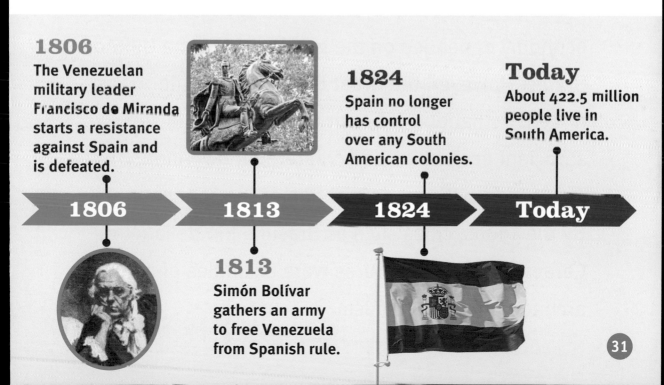

1806
The Venezuelan military leader Francisco de Miranda starts a resistance against Spain and is defeated.

1824
Spain no longer has control over any South American colonies.

Today
About 422.5 million people live in South America.

1806 · 1813 · 1824 · Today

1813
Simón Bolívar gathers an army to free Venezuela from Spanish rule.

New Nations, New Economies

In the beginning of the 20th century, South America's economy depended on the goods sold to the United States. However, the Great Depression of the 1930s forced the nations of South America to build self-sufficient economies and create their own industries. This sped up the modernization of the continent.

By the 1960s, cities such as Brasília, Rio de Janeiro, Caracas, and Buenos Aires were examples of modern architecture and urbanism.

A Chronicle From a Quechua

Felipe Guamán Poma de Ayala was a Quechua noble who wanted to inform the king of Spain about life in the Andes. He hoped to bring to the king's attention the injustices the Spaniards were committing against indigenous South Americans. Today, Guamán Poma's work is an important primary source about the Quechua people.

After the conquest of your Kingdom of the Indies of Peru, comes the rebellion against your royal crown . . . This work serves as a guide for the preservation of the Holy Catholic faith, to reform errors and help save the unfaithful for the salvation of their souls. . . . Your Majesty, I respectfully ask and greatly desire that you accept this humble service.

Guamán Poma converted to Catholicism after the arrival of the Spanish.

Here, Guamán Poma is referring to people who do not follow the Catholic religion.

The text Guamán Poma wrote was accompanied by drawings that depicted life in the Andes.

The letter has been adapted and shortened by Scholastic for young readers. Source: The First New Chronicle and Good Government *by Felipe Guamán Poma de Ayala.*

More than 12 million people live in São Paulo.

Commuters wait to board a train in São Paulo, Brazil.

CHAPTER 4

South America Today

South America has a population of 422.5 million people. They live in 12 independent countries as well as areas controlled by the United Kingdom and France. Among them are tens of millions of indigenous people and people with African roots. More than half of the people who live in South America are mestizos. This means they are of mixed indigenous, African, and European heritage.

Present-day Quito has a mixture of modern and colonial architecture.

From Cities to the Countryside

Many South Americans live in modern cities. Some of these cities still keep the colonial architecture brought from Europe. The biggest cities by population are São Paulo and Rio de Janeiro. Both are located in Brazil.

In some countries, such as Uruguay and Argentina, barely 10 percent of the population is rural. But in other countries, such as Ecuador, Bolivia, and Paraguay, about 40 percent live in rural areas. In rural areas, access to electricity and water is sometimes very limited.

Who's in Charge?

In the late 20th century, countries such as Argentina, Chile, Uruguay, and Brazil were ruled by military **dictatorships**. But today, most South American countries have democratic governments where people elect their leaders. In Suriname, the president is chosen by the elected National Assembly. Most South American countries have an elected president and an elected Congress, like the United States.

A woman from the small village of Laja, Bolivia, casts her vote in a presidential election.

The automobile industry is very strong in Brazil.

Economy

South America is rich in minerals such as gold and copper. The continent's farms supply much of the world's fruits and soybeans. South American countries also manufacture a wide variety of products, especially electronics, clothing, food, and airplanes. However, there is a big gap between the rich and the poor in most of the nations.

Made in South America

An export is a product that a country sells to other nations. This graph shows the top export for each of South America's four biggest countries.

Top Export by Country

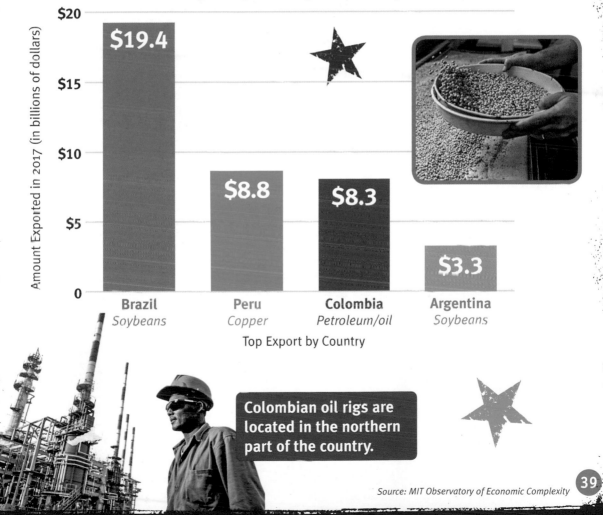

Top Export by Country

Y-axis: Amount Exported in 2017 (in billions of dollars)

- Brazil — Soybeans: $19.4
- Peru — Copper: $8.8
- Colombia — Petroleum/oil: $8.3
- Argentina — Soybeans: $3.3

Colombian oil rigs are located in the northern part of the country.

Source: MIT Observatory of Economic Complexity

39

Food and Sport

South America's cuisine is as diverse as its regions. In Uruguay and Argentina, people enjoy eating beef at barbecues called *asados*. Brazil's traditional meal is called *feijoada*. It consists of beans with beef and pork. Peruvian cuisine combines Andean potatoes and cereals with raw fresh fish.

One thing that unites the entire continent is a love for soccer. The teams of Brazil, Uruguay, and Argentina are always among the favorites to win the World Cup, an international soccer tournament held every four years.

South Americans of all ages love to play and watch soccer.

Almost two million people gather in the streets to dance and have fun during Rio's annual Carnival celebration.

Celebrations

South America hosts some of the biggest annual celebrations in the world. Carnival in Rio de Janeiro, Brazil, is one of the most famous parties around the globe. Countries such as Uruguay, Bolivia, and Colombia also celebrate Carnival, but Rio's event is the largest. Other important celebrations include Peru's Inti Raymi, an ancient Inca tradition. At Argentina's International Tango Festival, thousands of people gather to celebrate tango dancing. ★

Iguazu Falls
Argentina and Brazil

These majestic falls are the largest waterfall system in the world.

Salar de Uyuni
Bolivia

This is the world's largest salt flat. It is located high on the Andes at 11,995 feet (3,656 m) above sea level.

Destination

Perito Moreno Glacier
Argentina

Located in the Patagonia region, this glacier has a walking path that allows visitors to explore its icy surface.

Galápagos Islands
Ecuador

These islands are known for hosting many plants and animals that are not found anywhere else on Earth.

South America

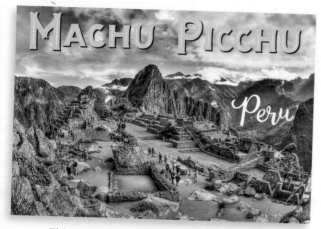

MACHU PICCHU

Peru

This ancient Inca site was constructed in the 15th century. It has been preserved as an important historical site.

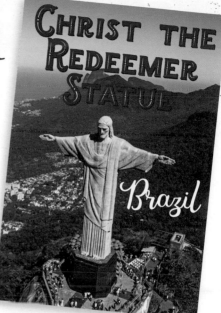

CHRIST THE REDEEMER STATUE

Brazil

This massive statue of Jesus is located at the top of Corcovado Mountain in the city of Rio de Janeiro. It is 98 feet tall (30 m), and its arms stretch 92 feet (28 m) wide.

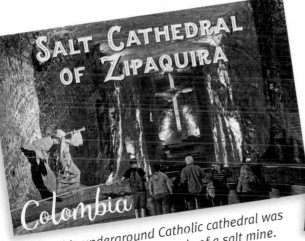

SALT CATHEDRAL OF ZIPAQUIRA

Colombia

This underground Catholic cathedral was built inside the tunnels of a salt mine.

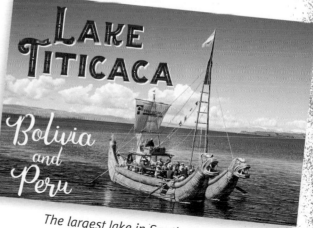

LAKE TITICACA

Bolivia and Peru

The largest lake in South America is located on top of the Andes.

Number of seats in Peru's Monumental Stadium, the largest sports arena in South America: 80,093

Height of Aconcagua, South America's tallest mountain: 22,837 ft. (6,961 m)

Population in Ushuaia, Argentina, the southernmost city in the world: 55,000

Population in São Paulo, Brazil, South America's most populous city: 12.1 million

Wingspan of the Andean condor, the largest flying bird in the world: 10 ft. (3 m)

Number of lightning strikes per minute near Venezuela's Catatumbo River during the peak of the rainy season: 28

Did you find the truth?

(T) South America has the driest desert in the world.

(F) Italian conquistadors were the first Europeans to arrive in South America and colonize its territory.

Resources

Books

Blashfield, Jean. *Argentina*. New York: Children's Press, 2015.

Brown, Risa. *South America*. Minneapolis: ABDO Publishing, 2014.

Mann, Charles C. *Before Columbus: The Americas of 1491*. New York: Atheneum Books for Young Readers, 2009.

Oachs, Emily Rose. *South America*. Minneapolis: Bellwether Media, 2016.

Williams, Rachel. *Atlas of Adventures*. New York: Wide Eyed Editions, 2015.

Yomtov, Nel. *Colombia*. New York: Children's Press, 2014.

Visit this Scholastic website for more information on South America:

★ www.factsfornow.scholastic.com
Enter the keywords **South America**

Important Words

biomes (BYE-ohmz) communities of plants and animals that have common characteristics suited for the environment where they exist

climates (KLYE-mits) the weather typical of places over a long period of time

colonies (KAH-luh-neez) territories that have been settled by people from another country and are controlled by that country

conquistadors (kahn-KEE-stuh-dorz) soldiers and explorers who conquered land around the world for Spain or Portugal

dictatorships (dik-TAY-tur-ships) governments led by rulers who have complete control over the country, often by force

habitat (HAB-ih-tat) the place where an animal or plant is usually found

indigenous (in-DIH-juh-nuhs) native to a particular area

migrated (MYE-gray-tid) moved from one region or habitat to another

plateaus (plah-TOHZ) areas of level ground that are higher than the surrounding area

temperate (TEM-pur-it) having a climate with temperatures that are rarely very high or very low

Index

Page numbers in **bold** indicate illustrations.

About the Author

Gloria Susana Esquivel is a Colombian writer. She holds a bachelor's degree in literature and a master's degree in creative writing in Spanish.